Introduction

So you're looking to start a wholesale business. Regardless of whether you're currently a white-collar professional, a business graduate looking to start your own business, or someone bored with their current job, starting a wholesale business is a great option. Much like the trading of the 18th century, you'll sell goods for profits. While the fantasy notion of standing on a harbor and bargaining over your shipment of fur is far-fetched, wholesale business has evolved hugely. If you're looking to become a wholesaler, then read this guide. Here, we'll talk about what's a wholesale business, key steps to run a wholesale business, and important considerations of wholesale for a small business.

Table of Contents

What is a wholesale business?

Wholesale refers to dealing in larger quantities or buying products in bulk directly from the manufacturer or distributor. In other words, a business that only buys and sells large quantities is a wholesale business. Manufacturers sell products in bulk quantities in most cases. The distributors buy the products at the company rate, wholesalers obtain them in bulk quantity at a low price, and then sell them to retailer stores or outlets. Once the products arrive in retail stores, end consumers buy them according to their needs. When you run a wholesale business, you are able to sell products for a lower price per unit because you’re selling in bulk. Wholesale businesses don’t have to spend too much on handling and other costs involved, thus it can be very profitable if done right.

Understand what is wholesale business

Before you let your mind weave an entire wholesale business plan it's important to understand its essence i.e. what is wholesale business?

Wholesalers are business entities that buy goods in bulk directly from manufacturers or distributors, and then sell them in smaller quantities to retailers.Although in modern times there are examples of B2C wholesaling, wholesalers per definition sell their goods to other business entities. This means their buyers are not the end consumers, but instead the retailers and similar business organizations the consumers buy from.Because wholesale businesses buy in bulk, they usually get special discounts and overall cheaper prices. In conclusion, wholesalers are sort of mediators between manufacturers and retailers. This puts them somewhere in the middle of the supply chain

Wholesale business examples

2020 is definitely not what we were hoping for. The optimism about entering a new decade has been smashed by the pandemic. Having that in mind, it would be crazy to suggest that products related to travel will sell well in 2020. This might have been the case last year, but not anymore. And since the situation is not settling down anytime soon, this list of wholesale business examples reflects the needs of humanity during a pandemic.

Home improvement products

We're all at home. Even after the lockdown eased up, we're still gravitating towards our home. So it’s no surprise that people have turned to renovations, DYI projects and home improvements. Considering that, the demand of home improvement products is rising and will continue to do so. Especially in the Northern Hemisphere where summer is at full speed.

Food

Food is something that has always been and always will be in demand. That’s for sure. However, food sales have hit record highs during the lockdown. And since people are still scared of a second wave, they won’t stop stockpiling. Especially not when autumn arrives and colder temperatures are on the horizon.

Electronics

Food is something that has always been and always will be in demand. That's for sure. However, food sales have hit record highs during the lockdown. And since people are still scared of a second wave, they won't stop stockpiling. Especially not when autumn arrives and colder temperatures are on the horizon.

Covid-19 essentials

COVID-19 essentials pop-up stores are the new thing. And these stores need supplies, so here's your entry ticket. It may feel like you'll be profiting from people's misery, but the truth is the bloody Coronavirus is everywhere around us and we will need face masks, hand sanitizers, thermometers etc. for a very long time.

Beauty products

I don't know who the first woman was, but I guess it all started from her. Women love beauty products. And as appears, in recent years men seem to like them too. There isn't a single celebrity left without their own beauty line: Lady Gaga, Kim Kardashian, Rihanna, Jennifer Lopez, Kylie Jenner,

Gwyneth Paltrow... The list goes on and on.

According to Forbes “The cosmetic industry is growing faster today than ever before with an estimated market value of almost $805 billion by 2023. It is expected to grow at a compound annual growth rate (CAGR) of 7.14% from 2018 to 2023.”

Backyard entertainment

I may have come up with that term on my own but trust me on this one. Borders are closed, travel is restricted. In other words, a lot of people won’t go on their traditional summer vacation this year. So they’re naturally looking for alternatives. A friend of mine recently wanted to buy an inflatable pool. And guess what: 6 stores he went to were out of stock! Add grilling, outdoor furniture, pool floats, sunbeds, umbrellas, lighting, sound equipment… to the equation and you have a ready-to-go wholesale business idea.

Fitness

As contradictory as it sounds, the most obese generation in history is also the most athletic one. Everyone's (at least trying to) eating healthy, exercising daily, jogging, meditating… Many during lockdown started exercising because they were afraid to get fat with all that food and staying at home.

Kids toys and educational materials

With the closing of many kinterdens, nursery schools, playgroups and maternal schools around the world, parents are practically held hostage. They are expected to work and take care of their children at the same time. The logical direction of this situation is that children need to entertain themselves and parents will buy all sorts of toys to have just one uninterrupted video call with their boss.

Organic goods

Organic this, organic that. Suddenly, the food, cosmetics, and consumer goods we used until yesterday are no good and causing all sorts of health problems. Several years ago it was hard to find a shelf in the deli with organic products, and now we have entire stores selling organic-only products.

Formulating a business plan is the key step for any new business. There are several steps here that are a must for a solid business plan.

The first step is market research. The study of the market trends and the state of the market is essential before starting a business. For a wholesale distribution business, you need to know about the leading players in the market in both distribution and the retail sides of the business. You need to study market trends and analyze them, read market studies on the distribution business, learn about profit projections of the retailers, and know your competition.

The second step is deciding on your specialization. For beginning stages of the business, it is wise to stick to one or two products lines or just a few products from different lines. For instance, if you like the idea of food distribution, you have the options to choose from fresh fruits and vegetables, frozen foods, dry foods, meat products, seafood, or dairy. You can choose 2-3 from the list or choose 2-3 from different, yet related lines such as stationary, books, school supplies, and so on. Specialization is important here, as it will help you focus on your core group and develop a solid foundation for your business. In fact, many successful distributors still deal with only a few products or products lines even after years of business. Specialization also helps develop relationship with a few manufacturers and retailers based on the product. These business relationships form an essential part or the backbone of a wholesale distribution business. Make a list of distributors and retail stores to do your business at the start with learn from about them.

Then, make the financial plan. For a distribution business, you will need warehouse space and transport facilities. Learn what will be profitable for you – leasing or buying. Add fuel costs, driver salary, and other overheads before calculating the approximate amount. Find out how much additional costs you will have to incur. Obtain money for buying your initial stock. Work out credit plans with the manufacturers or vendors and negotiate discounts. Know that you will need to buy large stocks to get big discounts from the manufactures. These discounts determine the profit margins of a wholesale distributor as retailers get the products at wholesale rates.

Apply for the permits and licenses if needed for your business.

Then, market your business and get organized. By this time, your business funds and leases and storage spaces must be in order. Print your business cards and meet your distributors and retailers. Join wholesale business networks and make new contacts. A small website won't hurt, either. In fact, a website can help a great deal in establishing a new distributing business.

Required skills

Wholesale distribution is a very competitive business. Find out if you have the necessary skills to begin and thrive in this trade.

For a wholesale distribution business, excellent negotiation skills are a must. This is the trade where distributors constantly need to work out the best rate to buy and then to sell the same product. This is where the money in this business is made. Negotiations are also needed to get access to promotional offers from vendors or manufacturers to pass them to the retailers. A distributor who arrives with good quality products and promotional offers is always a good deal for retailers.

Good organization skills in this business are always a boon. Keeping inventory, list of retailers, constant networking, buying stock, and daily upkeep of the business requires organization skills. The better you are at it, the easy it will be to run a wholesale distribution business.

Excellent communication skills are needed to form good working relationships. Manufacturers don’t offer the same discounts to all the distributors. Why one distributor gets a discount of 10% and another 12% depends on the nature of the working relationship. Communication skills also help in networking required in this business and navigating through this trade. A wholesale distributor needs to find new retail stores to do business with and this requires the work of research, analysis, and marketing over and over. A distributor also needs to look for new distributors who might sell a product in your existing line with better discounts. You might also need a new distributor for getting into another line of distribution business.

Money skills, knowledge of accounting, and good financial management will ensure success in this business. In the business of wholesale distribution, you need to constantly work with buying, selling, inventory, discounts, purchases, and credits. Without good knowledge of finances and accounting, it might become difficult to run this business.

Functions of a wholesale business

Buying

When you run a wholesale business, you are able to sell products for a lower price per unit because you're selling in bulk. Wholesale businesses don't have to spend too much on handling and other costs involved, thus can be very profitable if done right.

Warehousing and packaging

Because a wholesaler buys products in bulk, vast space is required to store the products until the demand is created in the market. In your warehouse, you may need to sub-classify the items into smaller packages.

Transportation

When you run a wholesale business, you may need to provide transportation as well. Transportation is used to deliver products to retail stores and outlets.

Types of wholesalers

Merchant wholesaler

A merchant wholesaler is the most common group of wholesalers, who deals with all sorts of products and usually takes title (ownership rights) to the merchandise they handle. Often related to the merchant wholesaler, the other participant in the wholesaling business is the agent and broker. Agents and brokers function as independent salespeople that facilitate the sales of merchandise between the merchant wholesaler and the retailer and get commissions when sales are made. Agents and brokers do not take possession of the goods, and that's how they differ from merchants.

Specialty wholesaler

As the name suggests, a specialty wholesaler is very specific about the type of product and industry. They might buy the product from multiple producers, but their core product remains the same.

Online wholesaler

Of all the types of wholesalers, this one is the latest entry. An online wholesaler sells products on an online B2B marketplace at a discounted price and in bulk quantities.

Dropshipping wholesaler

Leveraging an online platform, wholesalers can deliver products directly to the consumers. A dropshipping wholesaler can sign a contract with a retailer to operate smoothly.

The Distributor's Role

As you probably know, manufacturers produce products and retailers sell them to end users. A can of motor oil, for example, is manufactured and packaged, then sold to automobile owners through retail outlets and/or repair shops. In between, however, there are a few key operators-also known as distributors-that serve to move the product from manufacturer to market. Some are retail distributors, the kind that sell directly to consumers (end users). Others are known as merchant wholesale distributors; they buy products from the manufacturer or other source, then move them from their warehouses to companies that either want to resell the products to end users or use them in their own operations. According to U.S. Industry and Trade Outlook, published by The McGraw-Hill Companies and the U.S. Department of Commerce/International Trade Administration, wholesale trade includes establishments that sell products to retailers, merchants, contractors and/or industrial, institutional and commercial users. Wholesale distribution firms, which sell both durable goods (furniture, office equipment, industrial supplies and other goods that can be used repeatedly) and nondurable goods (printing and writing paper, groceries, chemicals and periodicals), don't sell to ultimate household consumers.

Three types of operations can perform the functions of wholesale trade: wholesale distributors; manufacturers' sales branches and offices; and agents, brokers and commission agents. As a wholesale distributor, you will probably run an independently owned and operated firm that buys and sells products of which you have taken ownership. Generally, such operations are run from one or more warehouses where inventory goods are received and later shipped to customers.Put simply, as the owner of a wholesale distributorship, you will be buying goods to sell at a profit, much like a retailer would. The only difference is that you'll be working in a business-to-business realm by selling to retail companies and other wholesale firms like your own, and not to the buying public. This is, however, somewhat of a traditional definition. For example, companies like Sam's Club and BJ's Warehouse have been using warehouse membership clubs, where consumers are able to buy at what appear to be wholesale prices, for some time now, thus blurring the lines. However, the traditional wholesale distributor is still the one who buys "from the source" and sells to a reseller.

Getting Into the Game

Today, total U.S. wholesale distributor sales are approximately $3.2 trillion. Since 1987, wholesale distributors' share of U.S. private industry gross domestic product (GDP) has remained steady at 7 percent, with segments ranging from grocery and food-service distributors (which make up 13 percent of the total, or $424.7 billion in revenues) to furniture and home furnishings wholesalers (comprising 2 percent of the total, or $48.7 billion in revenues). That's a big chunk of change, and one that you can tap into.

The field of wholesale distribution is a true buying and selling game-one that requires good negotiation skills, a nose for sniffing out the next "hot" item in your particular category, and keen salesmanship. The idea is to buy the product at a low price, then make a profit by tacking on a dollar amount that still makes the deal attractive to your customer.

Experts agree that to succeed in the wholesale distribution business, an individual should possess a varied job background. Most experts feel a sales background is necessary, as are the "people skills" that go with being an outside salesperson who hits the streets and/or picks up the phone and goes on a cold-calling spree to search for new customers.

In addition to sales skills, the owner of a new wholesale distribution company will need the operational skills necessary for running such a company. For example, finance and business management skills and experience are necessary, as is the ability to handle the "back end" (those activities that go on behind the scenes, like warehouse setup and organization, shipping and receiving, customer service, etc.). Of course, these back-end functions can also be handled by employees with experience in these areas if your budget allows.

"Operating very efficiently and turning your inventory over quickly are the keys to making money," says Adam Fein, president of Pembroke

Consulting Inc., a Philadelphia strategic consulting firm. "It's a service business that deals with business customers, as opposed to general consumers. The startup entrepreneur must be able to understand customer needs and learn how to serve them well."

According to Fein, hundreds of new wholesale distribution businesses are started every year, typically by ex-salespeople from larger distributors who break out on their own with a few clients in tow. "Whether they can grow the firm and really become a long-term entity is the much more difficult guess," says Fein. "Success in wholesale distribution involves moving from a customer service/sales orientation to the operational process of managing a very complex business."

Setting Up Shop

When it comes to setting up shop, your needs will vary according to what type of product you choose to specialize in. Someone could conceivably run a successful wholesale distribution business from their basement, but storage needs would eventually hamper the company's success. "If you're running a distribution company from home, then you're much more of a broker than a distributor," says Fein, noting that while a distributor takes title and legal ownership of the products, a broker simply facilitates the transfer of products. "However, through the use of the internet, there are some very interesting alternatives to becoming a distributor [who takes] physical possession of the product."

According to Fein, wholesale distribution companies are frequently started in areas where land is not too expensive and where buying or renting warehouse space is affordable. "Generally, wholesale distributors are not located in downtown shopping areas, but off the beaten path," says Fein. "If, for example, you're serving building or electrical contractors, you'll need to choose a location in close proximity to them in order to be accessible as they go about their jobs."

State of the Industry

Upon opening the doors of your wholesale distribution business, you will certainly find yourself in good company. To date, there are approximately 300,000 distributors in the United States, representing $3.2 trillion in annual revenues. Wholesale distribution contributes 7 percent to the value of the nation's private industry GDP, and most distribution channels are still highly fragmented and comprise many small, privately held companies. "My research shows that there are only 2,000 distributors in the United States with revenues greater than $100 million," comments Fein.

And that's not all: Every year, U.S. retail cash registers and online merchants ring up about $3.6 trillion in sales, and of that, about a quarter comes from general merchandise, apparel and furniture sales (GAF). This is a positive for wholesale distributors, who rely heavily on retailers as customers. To measure the scope of GAF, try to imagine every consumer item sold, then remove the cars, building materials and food. The rest, including computers, clothing, sports equipment and other items, fall into the GAF total. Such goods come directly from manufacturers or through wholesalers and brokers. Then they are sold in department, high-volume and specialty stores-all of which will make up your client base once you open the doors of your wholesale distribution firm.

All this is good news for the startup entrepreneur looking to launch a wholesale distribution company. However, there are a few dangers that you should be aware of. For starters, consolidation is rampant in this industry. Some sectors are contracting more quickly than others. For example, pharmaceutical wholesaling has consolidated more than just about any other sector, according to Fein. Since 1975, mergers and acquisitions have reduced the number of U.S. companies in that sector from 200 to about 50.

And the largest four companies control more than 80 percent of the distribution market.To combat the consolidation trend, many independent distributors are turning to the specialty market. "Many entrepreneurs are finding success by picking up the golden crumbs that are left on the table by the national companies," Fein says. "As distribution has evolved from a local to a regional to a national business, the national companies [can't or don't want to] cost-effectively service certain types of customers. Often, small customers get left behind or are just not [profitable] for the large distributors to serve."

Starting Out

For entrepreneurs looking to start their own wholesale distributorship, there are basically three avenues to choose from: buy an existing business, start from scratch or buy into a business opportunity. Buying an existing business can be costly and may even be risky, depending on the level of success and reputation of the distributorship you want to buy. The positive side of buying a business is that you can probably tap into the seller's knowledge bank, and you may even inherit his or her existing client base, which could prove extremely valuable.

The second option, starting from scratch, can also be costly, but it allows for a true "make or break it yourself" scenario that is guaranteed not to be preceded by an existing owner's reputation. On the downside, you will be building a reputation from scratch, which means lots of sales and marketing for at least the first two years or until your client base is large enough to reach critical mass.

The last option is perhaps the most risky, as all business opportunities must be thoroughly explored before any money or precious time is invested. However, the right opportunity can mean support, training and quick success if the originating company has already proven itself to be profitable, reputable and durable.

During the startup process, you'll also need to assess your own financial situation and decide if you're going to start your business on a full- or part-time basis. A full-time commitment probably means quicker success, mainly because you will be devoting all your time to the new company's success.Because the amount of startup capital necessary will be highly dependent on what you choose to sell, the numbers vary. For instance, an Ohio-based wholesale distributor of men's ties and belts started his company with $700 worth of closeout ties bought from the manufacturer and a few basic pieces of office equipment. At the higher end of the spectrum, a Virginia-based distributor of fine wines started with $1.5 million used mainly for inventory, a large warehouse, internal necessities (pallet racking, pallets, forklift), and a few Chevrolet Astro vans for delivery. Like most startups, the average wholesale distributor will need to be in business two to five years to be profitable. There are exceptions, of course. Take, for example, the ambitious entrepreneur who sets up his garage as a warehouse to stock full of small hand tools. Using his own vehicle and relying on the low overhead that his home provides, he could conceivably start making money within six to 12 months.

"Wholesale distribution is a very large segment of the economy and constitutes about 7 percent of the nation's GDP," says Pembroke Consulting Inc.'s Fein. "That said, there are many different subsegments and industries within the realm of wholesale distribution, and some offer much greater opportunities than others."

Among those subsegments are wholesale distributors that specialize in a unique niche (e.g., the distributor that sells specialty foods to grocery stores), larger distributors that sell everything from soup to nuts (e.g., the distributor with warehouses nationwide and a large stock of various, unrelated closeout items), and midsized distributors who choose an industry (hand tools, for example) and offer a variety of products to myriad customers.

Operations

A wholesale distributor's initial steps when venturing into the entrepreneurial landscape include defining a customer base and locating reliable sources of product. The latter will soon become commonly known as your "vendors" or "suppliers." The cornerstone of every distribution cycle, however, is the basic flow of product from manufacturer to distributor to customer. As a wholesale distributor, your position on that supply chain (a supply chain is a set of resources and processes that begins with the sourcing of raw material and extends through the delivery of items to the final consumer) will involve matching up the manufacturer and customer by obtaining quality products at a reasonable price and then selling them to the companies that need them. In its simplest form, distribution means purchasing a product from a source-usually a manufacturer, but sometimes another distributor-and selling it to your customer. As a wholesale distributor, you will specialize in selling to customers-and even other distributors-who are in the business of selling to end users (usually the general public). It's one of the purest examples of the business-to-business function, as opposed to a business-to-consumer function, in which companies sell to the general public.

Weighing It Out: Operating Costs

No two distribution companies are alike, and each has its own unique needs. The entrepreneur who is selling closeout T-shirts from his basement, for example, has very different startup financial needs than the one selling power tools from a warehouse in the middle of an industrial park.

Regardless of where a distributor sets up shop, some basic operating costs apply across the board. For starters, necessities like office space, a telephone, fax machine and personal computer will make up the core of your business. This means an office rental fee if you're working from anywhere but home, a telephone bill and ISP fees for getting on the internet.

No matter what type of products you plan to carry, you'll need some type of warehouse or storage space in which to store them; this means a leasing fee. Remember that if you lease a warehouse that has room for office space, you can combine both on one bill. If you're delivering locally, you'll also need an adequate vehicle to get around in. If your customer base is located further than 40 miles from your home base, then you'll also need to set up a working relationship with one or more shipping companies like UPS, FedEx or the U.S. Postal Service. Most distributors serve a mixed client base; some of the merchandise you move can be delivered via truck, while some will require shipping services

While they may sound a bit overwhelming, the above necessities don't always have to be expensive-especially not during the startup phase. For example, Keith Schwartz, owner of On Target Promotions, started his wholesale tie and belt distributorship from the corner of his living room. With no equipment other than a phone, fax machine and computer, he grew his company from the living room to the basement to the garage and then into a shared warehouse space (the entire process took five years). Today, the firm operates from a 50,000-square-foot distribution center in Warrensville Heights, Ohio. According to Schwartz, the firm has grown into a designer and importer of men's ties, belts, socks, wallets, photo frames and more.

To avoid liability early on in his entrepreneurial venture, Schwartz rented pallet space in someone else's warehouse, where he stored his closeout ties and belts. This meant lower overhead for the entrepreneur, along with no utility bills, leases or costly insurance policies in his name. In fact, it wasn't until he penned a deal with a Michigan distributor for a large project that he had to store product and relabel the closeout ties with his firm's own insignia. As a result, he finally rented a 1,000-square-foot warehouse space. But even that was shared, this time with another Ohio distributor. "I don't believe in having any liability if I don't have to have it," he says. "A warehouse is a liability."

The Day-to-Day Routine

Like many other businesses, wholesale distributors perform sales and marketing, accounting, shipping and receiving, and customer service functions on a daily basis. They also handle tasks like contacting existing and prospective customers, processing orders, supporting customers who need help with problems that may crop up, and doing market research (for example, who better than the "in the trenches" distributor to find out if a manufacturer's new product will be viable in a particular market?).

"One reason that wholesale distributors have increased their share of total wholesale sales is that they can perform these functions more effectively and efficiently than manufacturers or customers," comments Fein.

To handle all these tasks and whatever else may come their way during the course of the day, most distributors rely on specialized software packages that tackle such functions as inventory control, shipping and receiving, accounting, client management, and bar-coding (the application of computerized UPC codes to track inventory).

And while not every distributor has adopted the high-tech way of doing business, those who have are reaping the rewards of their investments. Redondo Beach, California-based yoga and fitness distributor YogaFit Inc., for example, has been slowly tweaking its automation strategy over the past few years, according to Beth Shaw, founder and president. Shaw says the 25-employee company sells through a website that tracks orders and manages inventory, and the company also makes use of networking among its various computers and a database management program to maintain and update client information. In business since 1994, Shaw says technology has helped increase productivity while cutting down on the amount of time spent on repetitive activities, such as entering addresses used to create mailing labels for catalogs and individual orders. Adds Shaw, "It's imperative that any new distributor realize from day one that technology will make their lives much, much easier."

Who Are Your Customers?

Because every company relies on a pool of customers to sell its products and/or services to, the next logical step in the startup process involves defining exactly who will be included in that pool. Defining this group early on will allow you to develop business strategies, define your mission or answer the question "why am I in business?" and tailor your operations to meet the needs of your customer base.

As a wholesale distributor, your choice of customers includes:

Retail businesses: This includes establishments like grocery stores, independent retail stores, large department stores and power retailers like Wal-Mart and Target.

Retail distributors: This includes the distributors who sell to those retailers that you may find impenetrable on your own. For example, if you can't "get in" at a power retailer like Wal-Mart, you may be able to sell to one of its distributors.

Exporters: These are companies that collect United States-manufactured goods and ship them overseas.

Other wholesale distributors: It's always best to buy from the source, but that isn't always possible, due to exclusive contracts and issues like one-time needs (e.g., a distributor who needs 10 hard hats for a customer who is particular about buying one brand). For this reason, wholesale distributors often find themselves selling to other distributors.

The federal government: Uncle Sam is always looking for items that wholesale distributors sell. In fact, for wholesale distributors, selling to the government presents a great opportunity. For the most part, it's a matter of filling out the appropriate forms and getting on a "bid list." After you become an official government supplier, the various buying agencies will either fax or e-mail you requests for bids for materials needed by schools, various agencies, shipyards and other facilities.

For a small wholesale distributor, there are some great advantages to selling to the government, but the process can also be challenging in that such orders often require a lengthy bidding process before any contracts are awarded. Since opening her Redondo Beach, California, distributorship in 1994, Beth Shaw of YogaFit Inc. says she's made several successful sales to the government. Currently, the firm sells its exercise education programs and several styles of yoga mats to Army bases and other entities. Calling government sales "a good avenue" for wholesale distributors, Shaw says it's also one that's often overlooked, "especially by small businesses."

Finding a Profitable Niche

Once you have done the necessary research on your soon-to-be customers and competitors, you will have a much better idea what type of niche your new company can fill. Profitable niches in today's wholesale distribution arena include, but are certainly not limited to, reselling products that require some degree of education on the seller's part. Take, for example, the pencil analogy: Selling traditional pencils is easy, but selling mechanical pencils that require a specific technique-and a refill-takes smarts. In the latter situation, a wholesale distributor comes in extremely handy because they can educate the customer, who can then educate his own end user, about the benefits and operations of the mechanical pencil.

In other words, what matters is not so much what you sell, but how you sell it. There are profitable opportunities in every industry-from beauty supplies to hand tools, beverages to snack foods. No matter what they're selling, wholesale distributors are discovering ways to reaffirm their value to suppliers and customers by revealing the superior service they have to offer, as well as the cost-saving efficiencies created by those services. This mind-set opens up a wealth of opportunities to provide greater attention to the individual needs of customers, a chance to develop margin growth, and greater flexibility in product offerings and diversification of the business.

The whole trick, of course, is to find that niche and make it work for you. In wholesale distribution, a niche is a particular area where your company can most excel and prosper-be it selling tie-dyed T-shirts, roller bearings or sneakers. While some entrepreneurs may find their niche in a diverse area (for example, closeout goods purchased from manufacturers), others may wish to specialize (unique barstools that will be sold to regional bars and pubs).

On the other side of the coin, too much product and geographical specialization can hamper success. Take the barstool example. Let's say you were going to go with this idea but that in six months you'd already sold as many barstools as you could to the customer base within a 50-mile radius of your location. At that point, you would want to diversify your offerings, perhaps adding other bar-related items like dartboards, pool cues and other types of chairs.

The decision is yours: You can go into the wholesale distribution arena with a full menu of goods or a limited selection. Usually, that decision will be based on your finances, the amount of time you'll be able to devote to the business, and the resources available to you. Regardless of the choices you make, remember that market research provides critical information that enables a business to successfully go to market, and wholesale distributors should do as much as they can-on an ongoing basis. It is better to do simple research routinely than to shell out a lot of money once on a big research information project that may quickly become outdated.

Pinpointing a Startup Number

While entrepreneurs in some industries seem to be able to raise money with a snap of their fingers, most have to take a more detailed approach to the process. Perhaps the best starting point is to figure out just how much you need.In the wholesale distribution sector, startup numbers vary widely, depending on what type of company you're starting, how much inventory will be necessary and what type of delivery systems you'll be using. For example, Keith Schwartz, who got his start selling belts and ties from his basement in Warrensville Heights, Ohio, started On Target Promotions with $700, while Don Mikovch, president of the wine distributor Borvin Beverage in

Alexandria, Virginia, required $1.5 million. While Schwartz worked from a desk and only needed a small area in which to store his goods, Mikovch required a large amount of specialized storage space for his wines-and a safe method of transporting the bottles to his retailers. The basic equipment needed for your wholesale distributorship will be highly dependent on what you choose to sell. If you plan to stock heavy items, then you should invest in a forklift (some run on fuel or propane, others are man-powered) to save yourself some strain. Pallets are useful for stocking and pallet racking is used to store the pallets and keep them in order for inventory purposes. For distributors who are sourcing, storing and selling bulky goods (such as floor tile, for example), a warehouse of sufficient size (based on the size of products you're selling and the amount of inventory you'll be stocking) is a necessity. To ensure that the distribution process operates smoothly, select a location that allows you to move around efficiently and that includes the necessary storage equipment (such as pallet racking, on which you can store pallets). Don't forget to leave room for a forklift to be able to maneuver between racks of pallets and shelves stored in the warehouse. As a startup distributor, your initial inventory investment will depend on what you're selling. Expect to carry some inventory, no matter what the product is, but also understand that your choice of goods will have some effect on how much you'll need to shell out upfront. Schwartz was buying surplus apparel, so $700 gave him plenty to work with for the first few months. When Garth Gordon and Vivienne Bramwell-Gordon, president and vice president, respectively, of Tampa, Florida-based Phones Etc., founded their company, they invested about $2,400 to purchase a shipment of high-end telephones. They quickly turned them around for a 300-percent profit and have been in the business of distributing refurbished Avaya telecom equipment to small companies and nonprofit groups ever since. Today, Phones Etc. carries about $600,000 in inventory at any given time. Bill Green, managing partner at WSG Partners LLC in Cherry Hill, New Jersey, says the best way to determine inventory needs is to look at your customers' needs. If they're the type who "need everything yesterday" (contractors working on job sites would fall into this category), then your inventory will need to be ample enough to meet those last-minute requests. However, if there's usually a three-to-four-day span between order-taking and delivery, then you may be able to skimp a bit on inventory and instead focus on forming solid, reliable relationships with vendors who can help you meet those timelines. "The most successful distributorships are the ones [whose owners] are working as close to their customers as possible and who can predict their needs and be there to provide value-along with the products," says Green. "That doesn't necessarily mean you need a huge warehouse and inventory, but you will need to find vendors who will 'hold' that inventory for you until your own customers ask for it."

Inventory Matters

In today's competitive business arena, companies are on perpetual diets. Owners and managers strive to run the leanest possible companies with the fewest employees and least amount of inventory and liabilities. In the distribution sector, some companies are being run with very low inventories-thus reducing their major sale (nonequipment) investments. Others choose to stock up in order to have "just what the customer ordered" on hand when the need arises.

There are caveats to both strategies. For starters, when a company chooses not to stock up, it runs the risk of being out of an item when the customer comes calling. At the same time, the distributors who overstock can find themselves in a real pickle if they can't get rid of merchandise they thought they could unload easily.

Being a distributor is all about "turning" inventory (selling everything you have in stock and then replenishing it)-the more times you can turn your inventory in a year, the more money you will make. Get the most turns by avoiding stocking items that may end up sitting in your warehouse for more than 90 days.

Stocking Up.Or Not?

How much inventory you buy at startup is going to depend heavily on exactly what you're selling, how far away your customers are located and how demanding they are. For example, if you're supplying customers within a 20-mile radius of your warehouse with janitorial goods like paper towels, rubber gloves and hand soap, then you can base your stocking quantities on the number of customers multiplied by an average usage by each. Their usage is most easily determined by asking them just how much they normally procure on a monthly basis.

On the other hand, if you are servicing a varied customer base located in different geographic areas, you may need to stock a little more than the entrepreneur in the previous example. Because you probably won't be visiting those customers at their locations, it may take a few months before you can determine just how much product they will be buying from you on a regular basis. Of course, you must also leave some breathing room for the "occasional" customer-the one who buys from you once a year and who will probably always catch you off guard. The good news is that having relationships with vendors can help fill those occasional needs quickly, even overnight or on the same day, if necessary.

"The biggest mistake companies make is developing an inventory load that is larger than what they really need," says Rich Sloan, co-founder of small-business consultancy StartupNation.com in Birmingham, Michigan. "The investment winds up sitting out in the warehouse when it could be put to much better use." Sloan says companies also jump into inventory purchases too quickly, without factoring in their customers' wants and needs-yet another way to wrap up too The distributor who has already invested in a location, vehicles and other necessities should also factor product life cycle into the inventory equation. Those with longer life cycles (hand tools, for example) are usually less risky to stock, while those with shorter life cycles (food, for examplc, usually has a short life cycle) can become a liability if there are too many of them on the shelf. The shorter the life cycle, the less product you'll want to have on hand. Ultimately, your goal will be to sell the product before having to pay for it. In other words, if you are buying computers, and if the manufacturer offers you 30-day payment terms, then you'll want to have less than 30 days' worth of inventory on the shelf. That way, you never end up "owning" the inventory and instead serve as a middleman between the company that's manufacturing and/or selling the product and the one that's buying it.

To sum up the tricks to stocking a wholesale distributorship:

Don't overdo it when it comes to buying inventory.

Try to get a grasp on your customers' needs before you invest in inventory.

If you can get away with doing it cheaply at first (especially those with low overhead), then go for it.

Be wary of investing too much in short-life-cycle products, which you may get stuck with if they don't sell right away.

Stock up to a level where you can sell the product before you have to pay for it.

For distributors, the biggest challenge is running your business on low operating profit margins. Adam Fein of Philadelphia-based Pembroke Consulting Inc. suggests making your operations as efficient as possible and turning inventory around as quickly as possible. "These are the keys to making money as a wholesale distributor," he says. And while the operating profit margins may be low for distributors, Fein says the projected growth of the industry is quite optimistic. In 2004, total sales of wholesaler-distributors reached $3.2 trillion, and for 2005 Fein expects revenue growth to continue to outpace the growth of the economy overall, growing an estimated 7.7 percent (vs. projected gross domestic product growth of 3.5 percent).

Playing the Markup Game

In its most basic form, wholesale distribution is all about the "spread," or profit margin, between what you bought the product for and what you sold it for. The bigger the spread, the bigger the profits. For example, in the wine business, Alexandria, Virginia-based Borvin Beverage achieves a 30 percent profit margin. People place great value on high-end wines, so they're willing to pay more for bottles of chardonnay than they will for, say, computer modems. Bill Green, managing partner at WSG Partners LLC in Cherry Hill, New Jersey, says the typical wholesale distributor achieves a 25 percent gross margin range, while those that offer "value-added" services are getting closer to 35 to 40 percent. At YogaFit Inc. in Redondo Beach, California, Beth Shaw says she strives for a 50 percent markup on all goods. That means the yoga mat that she buys from a supplier for $20 will be sold to her customer for $30.

Distributors can use the following formula when it comes to markup: If it costs the manufacturer $5 to produce the product and they have a 100 percent markup, then you (the distributor) buy it for $10. Following the same formula, the wholesaler would double the cost and sell it for

$20. Thus, there is a 400 percent markup from manufactured price to the wholesaler's customer.

Conclusion

Every successful wholesale business owner relies on marketing tactics that collectively create a solid strategy. Wholesale distribution is no different. By selecting ideas that fit your brand, you can build your own strategy to find and attract your ideal customers.

www.ingramcontent.com/pod-product-compliance
Ingram Content Group UK Ltd.
Pitfield, Milton Keynes, MK11 3LW, UK
UKHW021655190726
13853UKWH00001B/279